D1199241

Appaloosa Horses

Appaloosa Horses

Dorothy Hinshaw Patent
photographs by William Muñoz

HOLIDAY HOUSE / NEW YORK

To breeders who are dedicated to preserving
the true Appaloosa horse.

ACKNOWLEDGEMENTS

The author and photographer wish to thank George Hatley,
Kris Francis, Don Ulrich, Walt McDonald, Hugh Krantz,
Kelley Marler, and Jim and Judy Clairmont for their help
with this book.

LIBRARY OF CONGRESS
Library of Congress Cataloging-in-Publication Data
Patent, Dorothy Hinshaw.
Appaloosa horses / Dorothy Hinshaw Patent; photographs by William
Muñoz and others.— 1st ed.
p.   cm.
Includes index.
Bibliography: p.
Summary: Examines the origins, traits, and activities of this
spotted breed and discusses racing and breeding.
ISBN 0-8234-0706-3
1. Appaloosa horse—Juvenile literature.   [1. Appaloosa horse.
2. Horses.]   I. Muñoz, William, ill.   II. Title.
SF293.A7P38   1988
636.1'3—dc19   88-4470   CIP   AC
ISBN 0-8234-0706-3

Contents

Appaloosa Horses

Appaloosas graze in a pasture.

1

Indians and Horses

Indians and horses—we imagine them chasing after buffalo across the prairies. The horses are colorful, with splashes of brown or black on their galloping bodies. The Indians did love strikingly colored horses. Most tribes that wandered the Great Plains of the American West favored the pinto or paint, with its flashy black-and-white or brown-and-white coat. But two tribes—the Nez Perce (nez purse) and the Palouse (pah LOOSE)—preferred an equally colorful horse, one with smaller spots, that today is known as the Appaloosa (ap-pah-LOOSE-ah). The Appaloosa has become the fifth most numerous breed (after the Quarter Horse, Thoroughbred, Arabian and Standardbred) in the United States and is also becoming more and more favored in Canada, Mexico, Australia, and other countries.

Appaloosa Origins

Spotted horses have been around since prehistoric times. About 20,000 years ago, ancient artists drew images of spotted horses on the walls deep within two caves in France. In those days, horses were hunted for food like any other animal. The drawings probably were intended to help bring game to the hunters or to get the wild herds to multiply so food would be plentiful.

Those spotted horses, however, do not appear to have left descendants in Europe. The Appaloosas of today probably have their origins among the horses developed by tribes in the cold, treeless steppes of central Asia about 3,500 years ago. When horses were domesticated, it changed the lives of humans. With horses, people could wander from place to place on the backs of their mounts. Horses could carry their loads and pull their carts and chariots. Horses also provided meat, milk, and hides for leather. When mounted tribes descended upon peoples without horses, they defeated them easily. As a result of such invasions by tribes from Asia, horses became widely known in the Mediterranean region in ancient times, and art showing spotted horses appeared in Egypt and Greece in 1400 B.C. and in Italy and Austria in 800 B.C.

Horses came early to Persia (now Iran), which lies between central Asia and the Mediterranean lands. The great hero of Persian literature, Rustam, rode a spotted horse named Rakush. Rakush was chosen from thousands of

*The Persian hero Rustam, riding his spotted horse
Rakush, drags a Chinese ruler from his mount.*
COURTESY METROPOLITAN MUSEUM OF ART

horses brought from Persia, Arabia, and Afghanistan. In addition to being a great war horse, Rakush is said to have sired strong, beautiful spotted foals.

Spotted horses also reached China from central Asia, probably by 100 B.C. Before then, Chinese mounts were clearly inferior, with weak hooves and small size that made them no match in war for the central Asian horses. While all the superior western horses were valued, spotted ones were especially favored. When conquered tribes paid tribute to their Chinese rulers, they often gave spotted horses as part of the price of peace. Because of their value and beauty, spotted horses became common in Chinese art starting in the 7th century A.D.

Spotted horses paid in tribute to the Chinese emperor from western regions, painted during the 11th century by Li Lung-mein.
COURTESY FINE ARTS LIBRARY, UNIVERSITY OF MICHIGAN

Spotted horse in 1760 performing the arts of "haute ecole" (high school) riding, which are still carried out today by the Spanish Riding School in Vienna.

In western Europe, spotted horses appeared here and there during historic time but were specially bred only in a few places such as Denmark and Austria. The Austrians raised horses starting with Andalusian stock from Spain in the Lipizzan area of what is now Yugoslavia. The best were sent to the Spanish Riding School in Vienna, where they learned complex and beautiful movements. Today, all the famous Lipizzaner horses are born dark and turn white with age. But during the sixteenth to eighteenth centuries, many of them were spotted.

Spotted Horses in America

It was the Spanish who first brought horses to the American West. Since spotted horses were common among the sturdy Spanish Andalusian breed during the sixteenth century, they were almost certainly included among horses sent to Mexico during the Spanish conquests from 1519 to 1521. Some historians also believe that a special shipment of spotted horses was sent from the Adriatic port of Trieste to Veracruz, Mexico, near the United States border, around 1621. If so, they were probably especially fine Lipizzaners, which were being raised close to Trieste.

As the Spanish conquest spread, one of their explorers, Juan de Onate, was sent to conquer lands to the north of Mexico in 1598. A large number of soldiers and settlers accompanied him, bringing along 7,000 head of sheep, cattle, and horses. They took over the farmlands of the Pueblo Indians in New Mexico, turning the Indians into servants and slaves. The Spanish used horses to herd their headstrong longhorn cattle. The law prohibited Indians from riding horses. The Spanish knew that the Indians could be dangerous enemies once they learned how to ride and fight on horseback. But the Indians could see the value of horses. Now and then a trusted young Indian was probably taught how to ride to give a hand with chores that could only be done on horseback. In any case, the Indians learned bit by bit how to use horses.

In 1680, the Pueblos rebelled and succeeded in driving their Spanish conquerors south. By this time, some Indian tribes to the north already had mastered the use of horses, but the animals were hard to come by. They could only be obtained by stealing from the Spanish or by catching the few wild horses that had gotten loose from Spanish ranches. Horses weren't as useful to the Pueblo, who were farmers, as they were to the hunting Plains Indians, so the Pueblos' traded most of the horses they won from the Spanish to other tribes. This resulted in the rapid spread of the horse northward among the Indians. By 1710, Indians in the northwest were mounted.

Before horses came along, the Nez Perce Indians, who lived in the area where the states of Washington, Oregon, and Idaho now meet, dwelt in sturdy houses and fished for a living. Other northwest tribes who lived in regions with an abundance of fish were slow to take to the horse. But the fishing in the rivers where the Nez Perce lived wasn't especially good. The protected valleys among the rolling hills in the area, however, had green pastures ideal for horses. For these reasons, it was natural for the Nez Perce to take to raising horses.

Some of the Nez Perce did not adopt the new life, but most gave up their permanent settlements and began living in portable tipis, like the Plains Indians. They made trips across the mountains to the plains, where the buffalo wandered. With horses they could run down buffalo easily. Their buffalo hunting trips were occasions for adventure and social contacts with their allies, the Crow. While their journeys might last a couple of months, sometimes they stayed away for a year. The small, strong Nez Perce bow became a

Chief Looking Glass, one of the most important Nez Perce chiefs, on horseback during the 1870s. Note the stripes painted on the horse.
COURTESY SMITHSONIAN INSTITUTION

popular weapon among other tribes for killing buffalo.

The Nez Perce horses were also valued by other tribes. Unlike most other Indians, the Nez Perce chose which horses they allowed to breed. Only the best animals were allowed to mate and produce foals. This practice paid off by producing strong, swift horses that could travel long distances on sturdy legs and hard hooves. If a horse wasn't big, strong, or handsome enough, the Nez Perce traded it away, keeping the best horses for themselves.

The horses they kept were carefully divided among the people. The less valuable horses carried loads or were ridden by women and old people. The strongest and swiftest horses were used by the men, because a favorite sport of the men

Careful breeding can produce colorful spotted foals like this one.

was horse racing. When the tribes camped along the shores of the Palouse River, the men raced their horses along the flat meadow nearby while the women gathered and processed camas bulbs for food.

The most precious mounts were those ridden in war. The Indians liked to decorate their war horses with feathers, ribbons, and paint. The most important things for a war horse were speed, training, and courage. But flashy colors made it even more valuable. Spots of color were especially prized. Not only did they naturally decorate the animal, they also helped to camouflage it. The spots broke up the outline of the horse, making it harder to see at a distance.

From a distance, a spotted horse like this would be hard to see along the edge of the woods.

The Nez Perce favored horses with spots of brown or black on a white background or of white on a dark background. The explorer Meriwether Lewis was one of the first white men to encounter the Nez Perce horses, and he commented that many of their horses had unusual variegated coats, different from anything he had seen before.

Unfortunately, very little is actually known about these Indians and their horses. The only firm evidence that spotted horses were considered especially desirable comes from an interview with a Palouse Indian named Sam Fisher in 1946, when Mr. Fisher was 98 or 99 years old. The Palouse Indians lived near the Nez Perce and spoke the same language, but they considered themselves a separate tribe. Like the Nez Perce, they were fine horse breeders. Mr. Fisher recounted a ritual performed to help a mare produce a spotted foal. Three times during pregnancy, the breeder dipped his fingers in special paint. He placed his thumb on the mare's hip bone and spread out his fingers to mark the hip with spots. This act was supposed to increase the chances that the foal would bear the especially valued five-finger mark on its hip when born.

The name "Appaloosa" is derived from the original reference to a horse with spots as "A Palouse." The word "Palouse" referred to the tribe or to the river of that name. The Palouse River is a modest stream that flows through the rolling hills that once supported vast grazing herds but which now are blanketed by miles and miles of wheat fields. It originates in the mountains of southwestern Idaho and joins the Snake River in southeastern Washington in the heart of Palouse country. Early on, the spotted Indian mounts were

By marking a pregnant mare's hip with spots of paint, the Palouse Indian, hoped to get a nicely spotted foal like this one shown at the side of its mother.

*The Palouse hills where once Indian horses grazed are
now used to grow wheat and other grains.*

referred to by white men as "Palouse horses." This became
"A Palouse," referring to one horse, and then Apaloosie or
Apalousey.

The Lost Appaloosa

As white men settled the West, the Indians were forced to
give up much of their land. Some of the Nez Perce were
converted to Christianity, while others preferred to keep

their Indian beliefs. As more and more whites moved into Indian lands, increased pressure was put on the Indians to give up their old life style. The missionaries and government officials disapproved of the Indians raising horses. The missionaries didn't like the horse racing so loved by the Indians, nor the gambling that went along with it. The officials and missionaries knew that with horses, the Indians could more easily leave settlements and return to their old ways. They could also sell the horses and make money. With their own money, they were less dependent on the white men.

Some of the Nez Perce signed a treaty with the government to move to a reservation, but others refused. The government decided to try to force the bands that hadn't signed the treaty onto the reservation anyway. The largest and most powerful nontreaty band was led by Chief Joseph. These

Chief Joseph.
COURTESY SMITHSONIAN
INSTITUTION

Indians had several thousand horses and large herds of cattle. When the cavalry threatened to force them to the reservation, they traveled across the Snake River Canyon and Salmon River on their way to the reservation. The trip was dangerous, for both rivers were at flood stage.

Serious trouble began for the Indians when three young braves killed four white settlers. They had set out to avenge the murder of the father of one of the braves. This meant war, and the long battle between the Nez Perce and the army began. From June, 1877, through September, the Indians traveled from their homelands across the Bitterroot Mountains into what is now Montana, then south into modern-day Yellowstone Park. All along the way, they were pursued by the whites. Many battles were fought as the Indians tried to escape. Finally, refused help by their allies the

These Appaloosas in Wyoming are being raised only a few miles from the route the Nez Perce Indians took during their attempt to escape the U.S. cavalry.

Crow Indians, the Nez Perce headed north, hoping to find sanctuary in Canada. But while they were camped just a few miles south of the Canadian border, a surprise cavalry attack resulted in a six-day siege. The Indians lost and they were forced to surrender.

The whites promised to allow the Indians to return to their homelands, but after the surrender they refused to honor the promise. The Indians were eventually settled in what now is Oklahoma, far from their home, and all their remaining horses—about 1,100 of them—were surrendered to the whites. These animals had survived long, forced marches and incessant warfare; they were the best of the best and were sold to eastern buyers.

Meanwhile, the horses that the Indians had left back home were also claimed by whites. Some of these free-roaming Indian horses were caught during the winter by running them into snow drifts, while others were trapped at water-holes in the summer. Some settlers kept the horses they claimed, but others were sold to western ranchers. In this way, the proud breed of the Nez Perce and Palouse was disbanded. Not until 1938 would their descendants again be recognized as a distinctive breed.

2

Spots and Blankets

Just what makes the Appaloosa horse so special and different? For one thing, Appaloosas are valued for their gentle disposition making them good horses for children as well as adults. They are also known for their toughness. Some kinds of horses must be fed in the winter and carefully tended in the spring when the foals are born. But many Appaloosa breeders leave their horses out on the range throughout the year, even during the cold winter and at foaling time. But the characteristic that really sets these horses apart from other breeds is their coloration. Not only do Appaloosas have striking, colorful coats, they also have other color characteristics that aren't usually seen in other breeds.

The gentle Appaloosa is a good horse for children.

These Wyoming Appaloosas live outdoors in the pasture all year round.

Basic Appaloosa Traits

One trait shared by Appaloosas is parti-colored skin. Light skin is mixed with black, especially on the head, the rear, and under the belly. This is easiest to see on an Appaloosa that is predominantly white. While most of the hair is white, some of the skin under it is black, while other skin is white or pink. On some Appaloosas, the mottled skin is not limited to just the face, rear, and the belly. It shows up on the body, too, and the whole horse may be marked with scattered areas of white hairs with pink skin underneath.

The human eye is surrounded by a white area called the sclera. Most animals, including horses, do not have a white sclera. All of the eye that can be seen is dark. But like

Mottled skin on the face is a basic Appaloosa trait.

humans, Appaloosas have eyes surrounded by a white sclera. This whiteness around the eyes sometimes makes the horse look alarmed when it isn't. Other times, it gives their faces a human quality.

Finally, Appaloosas often have hooves with vertical stripes. Strips of dark hoof alternate with light areas. Sometimes the stripes are not clearly set apart, but the dark and light are obvious.

If a horse has these traits—mottled skin, white around the eye, and striped hooves—it is an Appaloosa even though it may not have spots. Such a horse can produce beautifully spotted foals even if it is bred to a solid-colored horse.

Appaloosas also often have a thin mane and a sparse tail.

These playful foals show the white sclera of the Appaloosa.

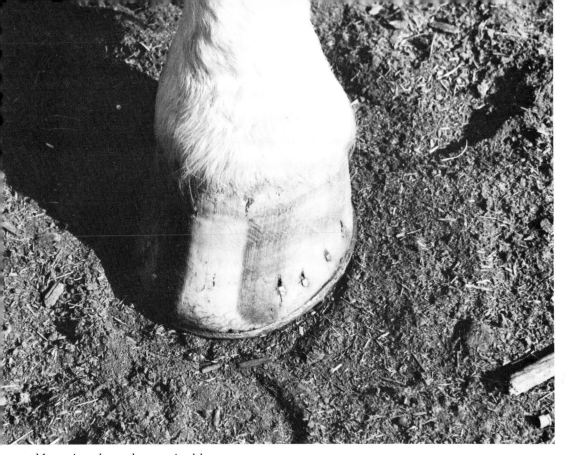

Many Appaloosas have striped hooves.

Appaloosas often have a thin mane and tail.

Because of the way the tail looks, it is sometimes called a "spike tail" or "rat tail."

Blankets and Spots

The famous Appaloosa spots come in different sizes and shapes. An Appaloosa can be white with a few big dark spots, or it may be dark, with tiny white flecks scattered all over. Some spots are round or oval, while others are pear-shaped like teardrops. The border may be definite, or the spot may be circled by an area of lighter hair. Small spots are often just a concentration of differently colored hairs, without a definite shape. When the horse grows its longer winter coat, the hair forming the spots may grow a bit longer than the surrounding fur, giving the coat a textured look.

The spots of colored hair may grow longer on the winter coat.

Perhaps the most familiar Appaloosa color pattern is the blanket. A horse with a blanket has a white area on the rump, often extending forward onto the body. The blanket may only cover part of one side, but most extend over both sides of the body. Most blankets are decorated with dark spots. But some are pure white with no spots at all.

Another familiar and especially striking Appaloosa pattern is the leopard. A leopard has a white coat over its entire body with large black and/or brown spots. Some leopards have round spots that look randomly scattered. But the spots of others are irregular in shape. Along the flank, or side of the horse toward the back, the spots are more concentrated and are shaped like upside down raindrops. This makes it look as if the spots had flowed up from the flank and out over the rest of the body.

Appaloosa with a spotted blanket.

A blanket with no spots.

A leopard.

*The spots on the side of this leopard foal look
as if they flowed up from its flank.*

A less common type of spotting is the snowflake pattern.
Instead of a white coat with large dark spots, a snowflake
Appaloosa has a dark coat with small, white spots. It looks as
if the horse had been caught in a snowstorm, and each flake
that touched its body had left a small, white mark.

A snowflake Appaloosa.

Roans

Many Appaloosas have a different color pattern called "roan." The word roan refers to a coat with white hairs mixed in with dark ones. In Appaloosas, the roaning is uneven over the body, and the horse is called a "varnish roan." Some areas are whiter than others, with more dark hairs over the parts of the body where the bones come near the surface. The hips, elbows, knees, and/or bones along the front of the face are darker than the rest of the body. The roaning may

A varnish roan.

just form a blanket over the hips or it can be present over the whole body.

Combinations of Colors

The different Appaloosa patterns can be combined with one another to form just about any combination. An Appaloosa with a blanket, for example, may have roan coloration over the front of its body instead of a solid color. White snowflake spots may be scattered amongst the roaning. The variety of Appaloosa colors and patterns makes them fascinating to watch. With so many possibilities, no two horses are ever exactly the same.

Changes with Time

Breeding Appaloosas for color can be very tricky. No one understands just how the different color patterns are inherited. Getting good color is often just a matter of luck.

This snowflake mare has a blanketed foal.

A white snowflake with small dark spots.

Not only can a breeder end up with a solid colored horse while hoping for a striking blanket, he or she might get a horse that starts with one pattern and changes with time. A varnish roan, for example, may begin with a solid color and only develop roaning as it gets older. The snowflake pattern can be even more confusing. A snowflake horse may start out solid and not get any spots until it is five years old. Then, after a few years with spots, the coat can change again, and the spots may be lost! Another snowflake might continue to get whiter and whiter until it changes from a dark horse with white spots to a white horse with dark spots. A few Appaloosas carry a gene for graying. Such a horse will turn whiter and whiter with age, even if it had loud colors when young. Only dark areas of skin will eventually remain to show where once there were colorful spots.

3

Appaloosa Activities

When the Nez Perce bred their horses, they wanted colorful, swift, surefooted animals that could be trusted on the
trail or warpath. The Appaloosa is still valued for these same
traits. Because it can run fast, the Appaloosa is popular for
racing today. Its surefootedness makes it a good trail horse
and a good cow horse, and its generally reliable disposition
puts it in demand as a family horse. All these traits are re-
flected in the variety of activities available for Appaloosas
and their owners.

Appaloosa Trail Rides

The Appaloosa Horse Club encourages members to share their love of spotted horses with one another by sponsoring trail rides in three parts of the country each year. Each lasts for five days. The Apache Land Ride in April takes place in Arizona. A hundred-and-fifty horses and riders go out each day from a base camp to explore the surrounding countryside. In the fall, the Sheltowee Ride in Kentucky is conducted in the same way.

The best known Appaloosa ride is the Chief Joseph Trail Ride in August, which commemorates the flight of the Nez Perce Indians from the U.S. cavalry in 1877. That trek ex-

Appaloosa trail riders head out.

tended over a distance of 1300 miles. Each year, a 100-mile segment of the trail is covered by about 300 horses and their riders. The ride must be carefully planned, as much of it takes place across rugged mountain country. The weekend before the ride, horses hauled from as far away as Kentucky and Tennessee and riders from all over the country gather at the starting point. The area is filled with the sight and sounds of spotted horses.

The club provides guides and meals along the way. The evening before the ride, everyone gathers to hear talks about the route of the ride, Indian history, and news of the club, and to meet their guides, followed by dancing and getting to know one another.

On the morning the ride begins, horses and people must be fed, and everyone saddles up for the journey ahead. Much of this ride is through some of the most beautiful country in the West, including parts of Yellowstone National Park and scenic mountain valleys. Twenty to 25 miles of trail are covered in five or six hours of riding each day.

The Chief Joseph Trail Ride gives Appaloosa lovers a chance to honor the history of the breed while enjoying a relaxing vacation shared with fine horses and good company. The riders who over the years cover the entire 1300-mile course of the trail receive a special plaque honoring their achievement.

Appaloosa Horse Shows

Humans enjoy competing with one another in many ways,

Getting breakfast before a long day's ride.

*Riders on the Chief Joseph Trail Ride proceed down the main street
of Cooke City, Montana, near Yellowstone National Park.*

one of which is to show off the animals they raise. Horses
are shown not just for fun, but also to increase their value. A
blue-ribbon animal is worth more for breeding or for selling.

Many events are featured at horse shows, especially those
for Appaloosas. Horse beauty, good training, riding ability,
and speed may all be tested during a weekend Appaloosa
horse show. The Indian heritage of the breed is honored by
classes for horse and rider in costume and by races run Indian style.

Halter Classes

Halter classes are the place to show off beautiful horses.

A costume class entry.

They compete against other animals of their same age and sex. The horses are judged on their conformation—how their bodies are put together. The way they move at a walk and trot is also taken into consideration, as are their manners. Even though striking color is important in Appaloosas, it is not a factor in judging regular halter classes. Some shows, however, do have a special class for the most colorful horse in which the animals are judged by their patterns.

Riding Classes

There are many different kinds of classes where horses are judged on how well they perform under saddle. In western pleasure classes, the rider dresses in western clothes and rides with a western saddle. In English pleasure, the rider wears traditional English riding clothes and uses an English

A judge looks over a foal at a horse show.

Western Pleasure Class.

English Pleasure Class.

saddle. When a horse is ridden western style, some of the cues it gets from the rider are different from those used in English riding. For example, the reins are used in different ways to tell the horse when to turn. Often, the same horse can perform well with both riding styles.

Trail Riding

A horse that is used either for recreational riding or on the ranch needs to be calm and cooperative when it faces unfamiliar obstacles. The trail riding classes test the ability of horses to deal with new circumstances and to be calm while the rider is doing things such as opening a gate or putting on a rain slicker. In a trail riding class, horse and rider must get through from six to ten obstacles. They must open a gate, pass through, and close it again. They have to ride over at

Trail Riding Class.

least four logs placed in the arena and walk over a wooden bridge. Other possible obstacles include walking through water, backing through markers, and staying quiet while the rider gets material from a mailbox. The trail riding class is a good test of a useful family riding horse.

Ranch Classes

Appaloosas are often used for ranch work such as rounding up cattle. And since it originated in the West, the Appaloosa has a tradition of western-style competition to follow. Several classes in Appaloosa shows test the speed and cooperativeness of a horse while working cattle. Separating a cow out from a herd and keeping it separate (cutting), and calf roping are favorite activities.

Races at Horse Shows

The Nez Perce loved to race their horses, and Appaloosa owners today enjoy racing, too. An Appaloosa show may feature one or more kinds of races. Like some other horse shows, Appaloosa shows may have barrel racing and pole bending, but they are run in a special way. The Appaloosa barrel race is called the "Camas Prairie Stump Race." Each course consists of a set of three barrels set 75 feet apart in a triangle. The horse and rider gallop down to the farthest barrel, wheel around it and head for the barrel to one side, circle it, and gallop to the third one. After going around the last barrel, they gallop to the finish line. In most horse shows, each horse-and-rider team goes through the course

A contestant tries to rope a calf's heel. One can see that his partner (out of the picture) has already roped its head.

Camas Prairie Stump Race.

once, and the one that gets through the fastest without knocking over a barrel wins. But at an Appaloosa show, two courses are set up facing in opposite directions. Two horse-and-rider teams race against one another. The winner of each heat moves on and races again against another winner. This continues until one horse and rider remain. If there are eight entries in the race, the winning horse will have to run the course three times. Thus stamina as well as speed is important in a winner.

The pole bending race at an Appaloosa show is called the "Nez Perce Stake Race." Two parallel courses of six stakes are set up, and two horses compete against each other in running to the farthest stake, then weaving their way down and back through the stakes, galloping to the finish line at the end. As with the Camas Prairie Stump Race, horses are eliminated until there is a winner.

Nez Perce Stake Race.

The rope race is like musical chairs on horseback. Ropes four feet long are tied to an overhead wire at one end of the area. There is one less rope than there are entrants in the race. Everyone races to the wire, and each rider grabs a rope. The slowest team won't get there in time and is eliminated. One rope is then removed, and the race is run over and over until only one rope and two teams are left. The rider of the fastest horse in the final race will grab the rope, thus determining the winner.

Rope race.

Young People at Horse Shows

Appaloosas are especially popular with children, so the shows feature many events just for young horsemen and horsewomen. They start out young, with a class for children under six years old. An adult leads the horse and young rider while the judge watches to see which children have the best riding form. Older children can compete against one another in the different kinds of riding classes. In addition to

This young rider is competing in the lead line class.

the riding classes offered for adults, young people can compete with one another in bareback riding.

One kind of race, called the keyhole race, is only run by children. A keyhole-shaped area is drawn in the ring. It has a twenty-foot circle with a four-foot opening. This narrow opening continues into a marked lane for ten feet in front of the circle. The horse and rider start at a line fifty to a hundred feet away from the entrance to the keyhole and must race into the marked lane, enter the circle and turn around inside, and gallop back through the lane to the finish line, all without the horse's feet touching the line around the keyhole.

Besides these events, children can enter showmanship classes, where emphasis is on how well the entrants show off the good points of their horses.

Bareback riding is a class for older children.

This horse and rider are turning inside the circle in the keyhole race.

Children can exhibit their showmanship skills at Appaloosa horse shows.

4

What Makes an Appaloosa?

From the surrender of Chief Joseph and the other Nez Perce in 1877, until 1938, there was no such thing as a recognized breed of Appaloosa horses. The Indian horses had been scattered far and wide, and their descendants carried out many different tasks for people such as herding cattle or pulling plows. Spotted horses were also popular in performances because of their flashy colors. Buffalo Bill Cody rode a spotted horse, and his wife rode in a carriage pulled by two more. Circuses used them as well.

In 1937, the magazine *Western Horseman* published an article by Francis Haines called "The Appaloosa, or Palouse Horse." Mr. Haines had studied the spotted horses and their history for many years. Readers were enthusiastic about the article, so the magazine carried more like it. Then, in 1938, fans of Appaloosas got together and formed the Appaloosa Horse Club. The club founders wanted to study the history of the Appaloosa and to establish a recognized breed.

Whenever a new breed of horse is established, many questions have to be settled. Each breed has a "registry," a listing of all the horses officially included in the breed. When a horse is registered, the owners can breed, show, and sell it as that kind of horse. Being registered makes a horse more valuable than one that isn't. With any breed of horse, it is important for the club to agree on how to decide which horses can be registered and which cannot. At first, standards for the breed have to be established. Then horses must be selected that meet those qualifications. These are the "foundation stock"—horses with the chosen traits that could be used in breeding.

When the Appaloosa Horse Club started out, the club officials had to rely on the word of breeders and on the photos of the horses to decide which to include as foundation stock. They started out by requiring that the horses have mottled skin, white around the eye, and striped hooves. They also classified the different kinds of spotting patterns that would be acceptable in the breed.

After setting these standards and registering foundation stock, the club officials had to decide which sorts of horses

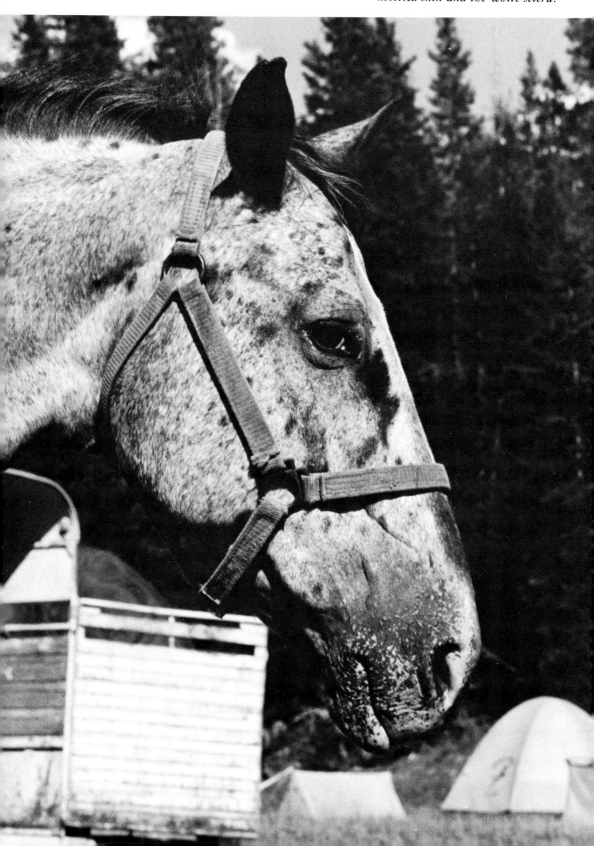

*This classic Appaloosa head shows both the
mottled skin and the white sclera.*

could be bred to registered Appaloosas to produce more Appaloosas. Besides breeding to other Appaloosas, crossing with Quarter Horses, Thoroughbreds, Arabians, and a few other breeds was allowed. As long as the resulting foal had

A promising Appaloosa foal.

the basic Appaloosa traits, it could be registered as an Appaloosa.

During the early years, keeping the club alive was difficult. World War II took people's time and attention, and developing a new breed of horse took a back seat to more important matters. But after the war, in 1947, the club moved to Moscow, Idaho, in the heart of Palouse country, and the breed began to grow. People had the leisure to go back in time and study the history of spotted horses. They learned that spotted horses had existed long ago. The discovery of the ancient history of spotted horses helped increase interest in the breed, and the Appaloosa was well on its way to becoming one of the most popular horses in America.

The Appaloosa Today

In recent years, Appaloosa breeders have argued about what makes a horse an Appaloosa. For a long time, a horse had to have mottled skin and a white sclera to be registered as an Appaloosa. It could only be entered in horse shows if it was clearly recognizable as an Appaloosa. Some breeders felt it was important to keep the Appaloosa breed pure and only bred their horses to other Appaloosas.

But many breeders liked crossing their Appaloosas to horses of other breeds. If a breeder wanted to produce horses for working with cattle, a cross with a Quarter Horse was a good idea. If racing was the goal, mixing in Thoroughbred blood could help.

This sort of breeding, however, resulted in problems. An

*This mare and her foal
are clearly Appaloosas.*

*Nowadays, a solid-colored horse without Appaloosa traits,
like this one, can be shown if it has Appaloosa breeding.*

owner might pay a lot of money to breed an Appaloosa mare to a champion Thoroughbred stallion. If the resulting foal lacked basic Appaloosa traits, it couldn't be registered as an Appaloosa. That meant that it couldn't be bred as an Appaloosa or raced to prove its speed and make it a valuable horse. All that money was lost. But that solid-colored horse might still carry hidden Appaloosa traits. If bred to an Ap-

paloosa with a patterned coat, it might well produce a foal that looked like an Appaloosa.

After several years of argument and changes in rules, the Appaloosa Horse Club finally settled on standards that answer most disagreements about what makes an Appaloosa. Now a solid-colored horse without mottled skin, white sclera, or striped hooves can be registered and shown as an Appaloosa. But when it comes to breeding, it must be mated with a registered horse with a patterned coat in order for the foal to be included in the breed. This allows solid-colored horses with Appaloosa breeding to compete as Appaloosas but maintains the long-term importance of coat color. After all, not all the Nez Perce horses were spotted.

Other rules have been changed, too. For example, instead of allowing breeding to a number of different breeds such as Morgans and Standardbreds, now only mating with registered Appaloosas, Thoroughbreds, Arabians, and Quarter Horses will be accepted. Limiting the kinds of horses used in breeding helps establish the Appaloosa as a particular type of horse, a colorful, athletic animal with many different uses.

5

Your Own Appaloosa

Appaloosas can be good riding horses. A well-bred Appaloosa can also be an easy-care horse. For example, the hooves of Appaloosas are sometimes tough enough that their owners never need to put horseshoes on them.

Kinds of Spotted Horses

Still, choosing a horse should be done carefully. Although Appaloosas are popular with children, sometimes a smaller horse is a better first mount. To be registered as an Appaloosa, a horse must be at least 14 hands high by the time it is

Choosing a horse to buy is a big decision.

A POA mare and foal.

full grown, at the age of five years. That means that the
distance from the ground to the withers, or top of the
shoulder, is at least 56 inches (one "hand" is four inches). If
an Appaloosa is shorter than that, it can be registered as an
Appaloosa pony. Rather than produce full-sized horses,

some breeders concentrate on raising the smaller Appaloosa ponies.

Another breed of pony with Appaloosa coloring is the Pony of the Americas, or POA. The POA was developed by crossing small Appaloosas, Quarter Horses, and Arabians.

An Appaloosa racehorse exercises on a "hot walker."

The goal was to produce an especially colorful and attractive pony for children.

What Horse to Choose

A family horse should be calm and reliable. It should be willing to obey anyone in the family and should not spook easily. For these reasons, a horse with little Thoroughbred

Appaloosa foals are playful and curious.

blood might be the safest choice. Thoroughbreds are bred to run fast and can be excitable, and Appaloosas bred for racing can have a lot of Thoroughbred blood.

The best way to buy any horse is to go directly to a reliable breeder. That way you can see what sort of home the animal has had and can see some of its relatives. You can talk to the person who raised and trained it, so you can learn something about its personality right from the start. A breeder is likely to try to sell you the kind of horse you want. He or she will want to please the customer to get good recommendations and repeat business.

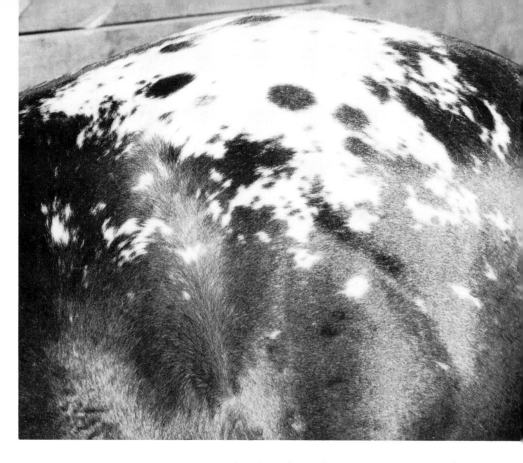

Appaloosa horses have a dazzling variety of spots.

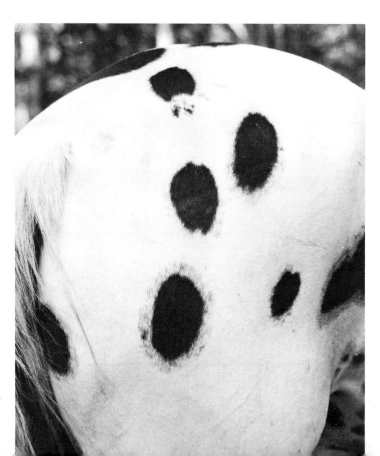

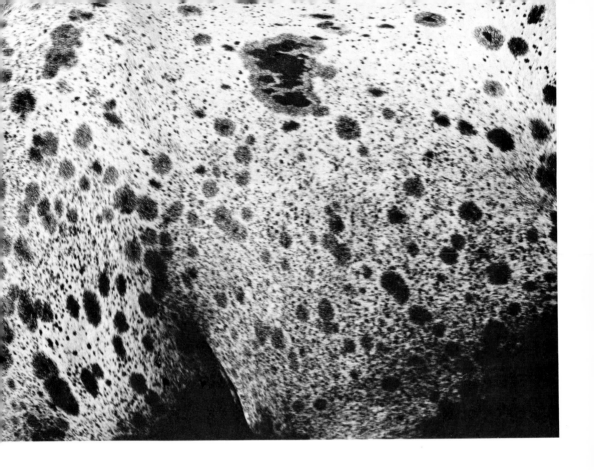

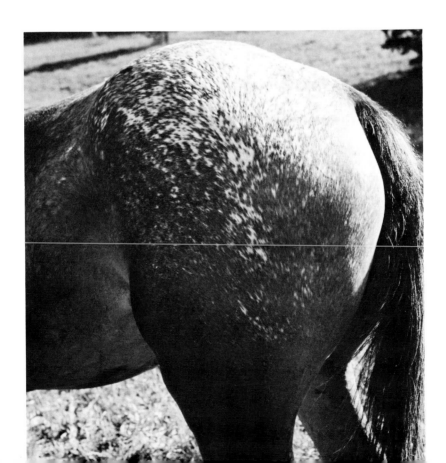

Appaloosas and Children

The Appaloosa Horse Club encourages young people to own Appaloosas by having many special activities for youths. There are shows, clinics in which children learn about horsemanship, and scholarships. Once a year, the *Appaloosa Journal* is devoted to youth activities, and other issues contain news about young Appaloosa owners. Many special awards for children who do well in shows help encourage participation, and each year there is a national show just for children and their horses.

For a child interested in developing his or her own skills and those of his or her horse, the colorful Appaloosa can be a good choice.

Sources for More Information

Appaloosa Horse Club, Inc.
P.O. Box 8403
Moscow, ID 83843

The official Appaloosa club

Appaloosa Color Breeders Association, Inc.
P.O. Box 456
Marion, KY 42064

Registers only horses with obvious Appaloosa traits

National Appaloosa Pony Club, Inc.
P.O. Box 206
Gaston, IN 47342

Registers ponies with Appaloosa traits

Pony of the Americas Club, Inc.
5240 Elmwood Ave.
Indianapolis, IN 46203

The Pony of the Americas is a distinct breed with Appaloosa coloring.

Glossary

blanket: A patch of white over the rump of an Appaloosa. The patch may be pure white, or it may have dark spots. The blanket may be over only part of the horse's rump, or it may extend along the back and sides toward the front.

calf roping: A timed contest in which the rider ropes a calf, dismounts, and ties the calf's legs together.

Camas Prairie Stump Race: The Appaloosa barrel race, in which a horse and rider are timed as they run a cloverleaf course around three barrels.

conformation: The physical appearance of an animal.

cutting: A horse's ability to separate a cow from a herd and keep it from returning to the herd.

English pleasure class: A competition in which a horse shows its training with an English saddle and bridle.

foal: A baby horse.

gallop: The fastest gait of a horse.

halter: A headpiece for a horse to which a lead rope can be attached.

halter class: A competition in which horses are judged on their conformation. The only thing a horse wears at this time is a halter.

hand: A measure of a horse's height. A hand is four inches. The height is taken by measuring the number of hands from the ground to the top of the withers.

keyhole race: A race for young riders in which the horse and rider gallop down to a keyhole-shaped area in an arena, turn around without touching the outline of the keyhole, and race back to the starting point.

leopard: A white Appaloosa with large dark spots scattered over its body.

mottled skin: Small areas of light and dark skin mixed in together. Mottled skin is an Appaloosa trait and is most often found on the face, the rear, and on the body between the hind legs of the horse.

Nez Perce Indians: An Indian tribe whose homeland lies in the area where Idaho, Oregon, and Washington now meet.

Nez Perce Stake Race: The Appaloosa version of a pole bending race in which two horses are timed as they run against each other, winding through a series of poles as fast as possible.

Palouse Indians: An Indian tribe that lived near the Nez Perce and spoke the same language, but considered itself separate from them.

pleasure class: A competition in which a horse shows how well it is trained for riding. The horse must obey the rider's commands when asked to change gaits, stop, back up, etc.

rat tail: A tail with thin, often short hair, typical of Appaloosa horses, also called a spike tail.

roan: Roaning refers to a coat with white hairs mixed in with dark ones. In the Appaloosa, the roan pattern (called a varnish roan) usually has more dark hairs over places where the bones are close to the surface, such as on the face, over the hip bones, and on the lower legs.

rope race: A race in Appaloosa horse shows in which entrants compete in galloping up to and grabbing ropes hanging from an overhead wire. There is one less rope than there are horses and riders. The race is rerun with one less horse and rider each round until one winner is left.

sclera: The part of the eye circling the iris. In Appaloosas, the sclera is typically white, as in humans.

snowflake: An Appaloosa color pattern in which a dark coat is speckled with small white spots.

spike tail: SEE rat tail.

trail riding class: Trail riding classes test horses in situations they are likely to encounter on the trail, such as keeping still while the rider opens a gate and dealing with objects that are unfamiliar to it.

varnish roan: SEE roan.

western pleasure class: A competition at horse shows in which a horse shows its training with a western saddle and bridle.

withers: The top of the shoulder of a horse.

Index

Numbers in *italics* refer to pages with photographs.